bhangra &
bollywood

Anna Claybourne

The website addresses (URLs) included in this book were valid at the time of going to press. However, because of the nature of the internet, it is possible that some addresses may have changed, or sites may have changed or closed down since publication. While the author and Publisher regret any inconvenience this may cause the readers, no responsibility for any such changes can be accepted by either the author or the Publisher.

First published in 2015 by Wayland

Dewey Number: 793.3'1954-dc22
ISBN: 978 0 7502 9438 6
Library ebook ISBN: 978 0 7502 7655 9

10 9 8 7 6 5 4 3 2 1

MIX
Paper from responsible sources
FSC® C104740
FSC
www.fsc.org

Concept by Joyce Bentley

Commissioned by Debbie Foy and Rasha Elsaeed

Produced for Wayland by Calcium
Designer: Paul Myerscough
Editor: Sarah Eason

Photographer: Adam Lawrence

Wayland

An imprint of
Hachette Children's Group
Part of Hodder & Stoughton
Carmelite House
50 Victoria Embankment
London EC4Y 0DZ

An Hachette UK Company
www.hachette.co.uk

www.hachettechildrens.co.uk

Every effort has been made to clear copyright. Should there be any inadvertent omission, please apply to the publisher for rectification.

Printed in China

Acknowledgements: Flickr: Christian Haugen 26–27, Adam Jones Ph.D 24b, killrbeez 26bl; Rex: Everett Collection 27tr, SNAP 18; Shutterstock: cinemafestival 2t, 6, 25r, Holbox 2–3, Kharidehal Abhirama Ashwin 3br, 30bc, Quayside 29cr, Smart-Foto 30bl, Testing cover, 10–11, 28tr, 28bl, 31br; Tamasha Theatre Company 2010: feastcreative.com/Barry Lewis 19.

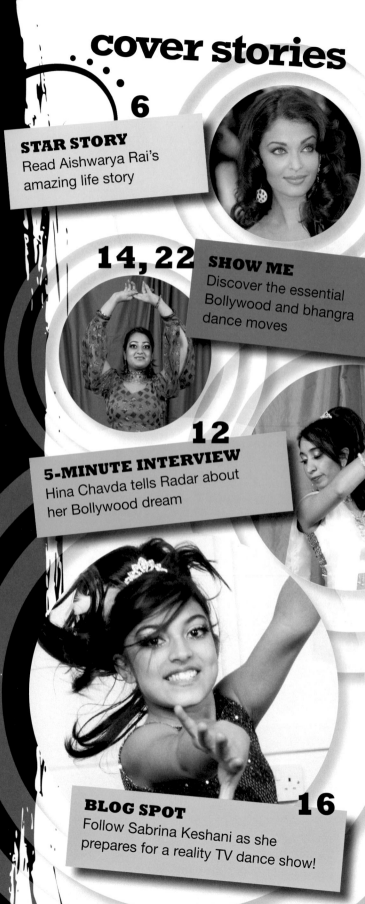

cover stories

6

STAR STORY
Read Aishwarya Rai's amazing life story

14, 22

SHOW ME
Discover the essential Bollywood and bhangra dance moves

12

5-MINUTE INTERVIEW
Hina Chavda tells Radar about her Bollywood dream

16

BLOG SPOT
Follow Sabrina Keshani as she prepares for a reality TV dance show!

thepeople

themoves

thetalk

BHANGRA & BOLLYWOOD

A whirlwind of music and moves, mesmerising beats and swirling, colourful costumes – the trademark features of Bollywood and bhangra dance are unmistakable. These spectacular dances began in India, then exploded onto the big screen in Bollywood movies.

Bombay blockbusters

Bollywood is the name for the Indian musical film industry, which is based in Mumbai, India. Mumbai used to be called Bombay, and the word 'Bollywood' comes from combining the letter 'B' (for Bombay) with 'Hollywood'. Bollywood churns out blockbusting, crowd-pulling films that feature the very best of Indian song and dance.

East meets west

Bollywood dance is an exciting blend of many different eastern and western dance styles. In this rhythmic melting pot almost anything and everything goes! Bollywood routines are a fascinating mix of dance forms, from bhangra and Indian classical moves to belly dancing, street dance, jazz, pop and even Latin dance!

Bhangra beat

This traditional Indian dance began as a folk dance, performed to the beat of a drum called a dhol. It was used to celebrate a good harvest. Modern bhangra is a bopping mix of this traditional folk-dance style with other music and dance, such as pop, hip-hop and breakdancing.

A spicy mix

Bollywood films are fusions of dance, music and dramatic plot lines all rolled into one breathtaking cinema experience. These exotic extravaganzas are sometimes called 'massala movies' because, like the massala spice mixture, they contain a 'bit of everything'!

Type 'Bollywood dance' into www.youtube.com to see what the Bollywood buzz is all about.

AISHWARYA RAI

The Queen of Bollywood

THE STATS

Name: Aishwarya Rai
Born: 1 November 1973
Place of birth: Mangalore, India
Job: Actress and model

Bright and beautiful

Aishwarya's family moved from Mangalore to Mumbai when she was four years old. Aishwarya worked hard at school and planned to become an architect when she grew up. Not only was she bright, Aishwarya was also stunningly beautiful. As a teenager, she started modelling just to earn some money, then, in 1994, Aishwarya entered the Miss World contest. Her striking looks won her the crown and overnight fame followed!

Camera, lights, action!

Miss World made Aishwarya a household name, but it was her acting and dancing that turned her into a superstar. In 1997, she starred in her very first film, *The Duo (Iruvar)*. The film was a massive hit and won several awards, so it wasn't long before great Bollywood film directors were clamouring for Aishwarya's attention. In 1999 she starred in the Bollywood blockbuster *Straight From the Heart (Hum Dil De Chuke Sanam)* and scooped the Best Actress award at the Hindi film industry's famous Filmfare Awards.

Queen of the screen

In 2004 Aishwarya wowed international audiences in the Bollywood-style English movie *Bride and Prejudice*. Three years later she married fellow Bollywood star Abhishek Bachchan in Mumbai. The glamorous couple attracted huge media attention across India and quickly became known as 'Bollywood royalty'. Today, Aishwarya's fame has spread worldwide and the undisputed 'Queen of Bollywood' is an international superstar.

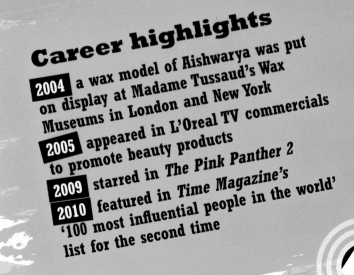

Career highlights

2004 a wax model of Aishwarya was put on display at Madame Tussaud's Wax Museums in London and New York

2005 appeared in L'Oreal TV commercials to promote beauty products

2009 starred in *The Pink Panther 2*

2010 featured in *Time Magazine's* '100 most influential people in the world' list for the second time

RISING STAR

My story by Danika Patel

I've always loved dancing and could tap and ballet dance at the age of five! Soon after this, a friend joined a Bollywood dance group and asked me if I wanted to give it a go. It was so much fun! I loved everything about it, from the music and dance to the gorgeous clothes.

I did my first Bollywood dance show at an arts festival when I was still just five years old. It was really scary. There were so many people in the audience and on stage that I freaked out and ran off the stage after the dance! Looking back it was a bit embarrassing, I guess. Somehow I got my nerves back under control for my next show, performing at the *Mega Mela* (an event celebrating Indian culture) in front of hundreds of people. After the show one of the most famous Bollywood actresses ever, Juhi Chawla, asked to meet my dance group. She called us 'the little chipmunks' and said we were cute!

When I was seven years old all of my hard work paid off when my dance troupe entered our first *Britain's Got Talent* competition. We entered as two separate groups – one for the kids and one for the adults. But when the adult group went on stage, Simon Cowell told them to stop halfway through their act. He knew about our kids' group and asked the adults to do a routine with us as one big group. We were in total panic – we had just one day to come up with a perfect new routine! But at the audition we were step-perfect and got through to the next round. One of the judges, Amanda Holden, said we were 'sparkling and magical'!

Four years on and we are auditioning for *Britain's Got Talent* again. I have my hopes pinned on making it to the finals this time. Bollywood dance has given me so much confidence, taught me new things about Indian culture and, best of all, I've made the greatest friends you could ever have – my Bollywood dance troupe.

DanikaP

BOLLYWOOD DREAMS

The silk of your costume swishes like a cloud of gold as you shake your wrist bangles to signal the start of your dance. Bright lights shimmer and the camera lenses lean towards your swaying body. Around you other dancers begin to move, their make-up and sequins glitter like a thousand stars under the dazzling lights. But you are the star of the show and all eyes are on you.

Here comes the rhythm

The bhangra drum pounds like a beating heart. At first the rhythm is slow and your body sways in time to the music. Then the pace picks up, and your body responds. You pound your feet on the floor and circle your hips. Then your arms reach towards the light, snaking through the air like serpents while you ripple your wrists and fingers. Then the set comes alive as dancers stamp, leap and whirl like spinning tops across the floor.

Can't stop the beat

Colours rush before your eyes. The dancers shimmer as their gold, red, purple and orange saris create a rainbow of intense colours. The sounds of the sitar and drum grow louder and the moves get faster. Now the dance crew surrounds you in a circle, feet drum the floor and a curtain of arms wave through the air. The director yells 'cut', but nothing can stop the beat – this is Bollywood at its best.

All singing and dancing

Bollywood actors mime to a pre-recorded song as they dance. They must time their words, hand and feet movements and facial expressions perfectly to match the beat of the music and the sounds of the recording.

HINA CHAVDA

Professional Bollywood and bhangra dancer and choreographer Hina Chavda tells Radar what makes Indian dance such a red-hot sensation!

When did you get into Bollywood dance?

I learned classical Indian dance until I was 12 years old and so mastered the basic techniques that you need for all Indian dances. Soon after that I discovered Bollywood dancing, and I loved it straight away!

Why is Bollywood so popular in the West today?

I think the fantasy and escapism of Bollywood dances and films appeal to western audiences. Shilpa Shetty's appearance on the TV reality show *Big Brother* had a big effect, too – it made people really start to take notice of Bollywood stars!

Have you met any celebrities while dancing or teaching?

I met the Bollywood film stars Shahrukh Khan and Shilpa Shetty at a Bollywood dance event. My dance troupe also put on a performance at a charity dinner held by *Dragon's Den* star James Caan. He really loved our show!

Have you worked in the bhangra music scene?

I've worked with both British and international bhangra artists, including Raghav, Malkit Singh, B21, Apache Indian, Hunterz and Roach Killa – just to name a few! I've helped to choreograph bhangra dance routines for their music videos, which was a fantastic experience for me.

Who is the most unlikely person you've taught dance to?

I taught Richard Branson to bhangra dance when we performed in the VIP lounge at Heathrow Airport to celebrate the first Virgin Airlines flight to Delhi! We also danced with Gordon Ramsay at a *Comic Relief* event in London, which was great fun. I think Gordon liked it, too!

Who do you think are the best Bollywood dancers of today?

Aishwarya Rai (see pages 6–7) and Madhuri Dixit are amazing dancers. They both trained in Kathak (a classical Indian dance) and learned from Birju Maharak, India's most famous Kathak dancer. He taught my teacher's teacher's teacher! He is known as the King of Kathak.

WAVE AND ROW

This simple move is popular in lots of bhangra dance routines. When put to music, the dancer appears to 'row', 'wave' and 'spin' in time to the beat!

You will need:

- **comfortable clothes** • **bare feet**
- **space to dance in** • **bhangra music**

Type 'bhangra dances' into www.youtube.com to see other great bhangra dances in action.

1

Step forward with your right foot and swing your arms to the left of your waist to 'row'.

2

Step forward with your left foot and swing your arms to the right, to 'row' once more.

3

Step forward again with your right foot. Raise your arms above your head and swing them to the left to 'wave'.

5

Hold your arms at right angles. Spin anticlockwise on your left foot, making a complete circle with your right foot – as if 'touching' the numbers 12, 9, 6 and 3 on a clock face. At the same time, curl and uncurl your hands as you make the spin. When your foot touches the number 3, spin back clockwise until your foot touches number 12 again!

Step forward... left foot. Raise your arms above your head and swing them to the right to 'wave'.

Got it?

You should have moved in time to the beat of the music, making a flowing sequence of 'rows', 'waves' and 'spins'. You should have curled and uncurled the palms of your hands with each 'point' of the clock on your spins.

A WEEK IN THE LIFE OF BUDDING DANCE STAR

SABRINA KESHANI

blog   news   events

Monday

It's only five days to go until the *Britain's Got Talent* auditions – I'm really excited, but a bit scared, too! We put in a really long training session after school today to get ready. We've GOT to get through the auditions to the live show this year, so our Bollywood dance routine must be perfect.

Tuesday

I had everyone laughing when I did a bit of Bollywood dancing in my drama class tonight. But, hey, I've got to showcase my dance style anytime, anywhere! When I got home, I ate dinner and then practised my routine once more.

Wednesday

No afterschool clubs or Bollywood classes today, so I just chilled out at home. I watched a bit of TV, did my homework and emailed my friends. They all wished me luck for Saturday's big audition. Thanks, guys!

Friday

My friend from the dance team came over to stay tonight – we are going to the auditions together tomorrow. We packed our costumes and ran through our routine one more time. Then we tried to go to sleep early – no chance! We were too excited (and too nervous) to sleep, so we stayed up chatting instead. Luckily Mum couldn't hear us!

Saturday

Yawn! We were so tired today. We had to get up at 6.30am to head to the audition in Birmingham. When we arrived it took an hour and a half to get the team's hair and make-up done! It seemed like ages until we were called on stage, and we all waited nervously, then, two and a half minutes later, our audition was over! It went really well, but we won't know if we are through to the next round for a couple of months. If we do get through it will be totally AMAZING! National stardom, bring it on!

EXOTIC HEIGHTS

What happens when you take a world-famous nineteenth century English novel, filled with tragedy and misfortune, and mix it up with a generous dash of Bollywood spice? The Asian theatre company Tamasha has done just that in its stage production of *Wuthering Heights*, transporting the original dramatic story to an Indian landscape, and adding saris, vibrant song-and-dance sets and a cast that could have stepped straight out of a Bollywood movie!

The 1939 film *Wuthering Heights*, starring Laurence Olivier and Merle Oberon, provided inspiration for Tamasha's stage production.

Mixing it up

But fusing eastern and western style is nothing new, as Bollywood style and western literature have already been mixed together on the big screen. Jane Austen's *Pride and Prejudice* was given a Bollywood make-over in the 2004 film *Bride and Prejudice*, which starred Bollywood superstar Aishwarya Rai. Baz Luhrmann also recreated the glitz and glamour of Bollywood movies in his spectacular Hollywood musical, *Moulin Rouge*. So when Tamasha's artistic director, Kristine Landon-Smith, and writer Deepak Verma got together they saw that a Bollywood version of *Wuthering Heights* would make a magical stage production.

A Bollywood dream

Emily Brontë's original story, featuring tragic couple Cathy and Heathcliff, has all the drama, intensity and passion of a Bollywood blockbuster. So transporting the epic tale from the windswept Yorkshire moors to the banks of the River Ganges in India made perfect sense to Kristine: 'It's such a perfect marriage of story and genre, it seems almost obvious.'

Tamasha's interpretation of the classic *Wuthering Heights* is a vibrant cocktail of dance, music and storytelling – resulting in a delicious mix of cultures. So if you want to see what Bollywood brings to Brontë, head to a production near you!

Tamasha's *Wuthering Heights* is set in Rajastan, India, in the nineteenth century. The play swaps windswept moors for deserts and camels, and Heathcliff is renamed 'Krishan' and Cathy 'Shakuntala', but the plot storyline remains faithful to the original novel.

To find out more type 'Tamasha *Wuthering Heights*' into www.youtube.com.

19

the lightbulb

wash the windows

20

THE MOVES

Bollywood and bhangra dances are flamboyant and rhythmic. Routines are made up of a variety of dance moves that are seamlessly pieced together. Here is a taster of some basic moves.

Type 'Bollywood dance steps' into www.youtube.com to see simple Bollywood dance moves.

The lightbulb

This classic bhangra move is often used in Bollywood dance sets. The dancer holds one arm in the air above their head and twists the wrist, as if unscrewing a lightbulb! At the same time, they wiggle the hips and bounce on the balls of the feet in time to the music.

The drive

The dancer holds the left arm in front of the body, as if holding the steering wheel of a car. With the right hand, they punch above and below the left arm as they shake the head from side to side and wiggle the hips.

Wash the windows

Both arms are held above the head. The dancer reaches the right arm to the side, and bends the left arm at the elbow, so that the palm faces upward. They then switch sides, to reach the left arm to the side and bend the right arm at the elbow. The dancer bounces on the balls of the feet in time to the music.

The lotus

One of the most famous of all Bollywood dance moves, the lotus is also one of the most eye-catching. The lead dancer stands at the front of the group, with the remaining dancers in a line behind her. The lead dancer holds her arms out to the side, while the remaining dancers also hold their arms out in varying positions. This creates a 'fan' of arms around the lead dancer and a shape that resembles a lotus flower.

APPLE, FLOWER

Type 'Bollywood dance basics' into www.youtube.com to see some other basic Bollywood dance moves.

Pick 'apples' and 'flowers' with this simple Bollywood dance move! You 'pick' apples as you swing your arms above your head and flowers when you sweep your arms below your waist.

You will need:

- **comfortable clothes** • **bare feet**
- **space to dance in** • **dance music**

1

Place your right foot in front of your left foot. Lean to the right and swing your arms to your left.

2

Place your left foot in front of your right foot. Lean to the left and swing your arms to the right. 'Pick' a flower by touching your index finger to your thumb.

3 Step to the left with your left foot. Place your left hand on your hip and reach up with your right hand. 'Pick' an apple.

4 Swap positions to put your right hand on your hip and reach up with your left arm to 'pick' another apple.

Got it?

As you 'picked' the flowers and apples your index finger and thumb of the picking hand should have been held together. Once you have mastered the move, you can start to perform it to music with a fast beat – and pick a lot more apples and flowers!

THE BOLLYWOOD STORY

Bhangra and Bollywood dances are an explosive mix of east meets west. British people arrived in India during the 1600s and by the 1850s they controlled most of the country as part of the British Empire. India started to gain independence throughout the 1900s, but during their stay the British had left their mark on much of Indian culture, from dance and music to its blossoming film industry.

Bollywood begins

The first Bollywood-style Indian film, with sound and songs, was Ardeshir Irani's *The Light of the World* (*Alam Ara)* in 1931. This was a love story about a beautiful gypsy girl, Alam Ara, and a handsome Indian prince. The film was so popular with film audiences when it launched that police had to be brought in to control the crowds!

The golden age

From the 1940s to the 1960s, Bollywood concentrated on producing lavish films that tackled issues such as mass poverty and working class life in Indian cities. These films helped ordinary people deal with problems in their own lives. Many of the films produced during this 'golden age' of film-making are recognised today as some of the greatest of all Bollywood films. In 1946 the film *Lowly City (Neecha Nagar)* won the Grand prize at the first Cannes Film Festival in France. Bollywood had arrived in the west!

All that glitters

The decade of the 'swinging 60s' hit Bollywood in a big way. Suddenly, romance and action films were big news. Film sets became more dazzling, the costumes became more flamboyant and the dance routines and music became more spectacular. These fun, fantastical and action-packed movies drew the crowds and made great sums of money for the studios and stars. To this day, Bollywood remains famous for its glittering, glamorous, larger-than-life movies.

Today, Bollywood stars hit the red carpet with Hollywood actors and actresses. Here Bollywood meets Hollywood as stunning actress Aishwarya Rai rubs shoulders with US actress Eva Longoria.

Heading west

During the 1980s and 1990s western pop music became even more influential in India, thanks to TV and music channels such as MTV. West and east started to join up, with Bollywood films featuring western culture, and western culture featuring Bollywood style. Meanwhile, Bollywood dance classes sprang up all over the globe, bringing the bhangra beat to millions of people who had grown up with rock and pop. Colourful and sensational, Bollywood really is the new Hollywood – and it's here to stay!

BOLLYWOOD BEST!

It's over 80 years since the first Bollywood film hit India's big screen and in that time, many blockbusting movies have been made. Here's Radar's guide to the most successful Bollywood films.

1

Mother India (Bharat Mata)

Released: 1957

Starring: Nargis, Sunil Dutt, Rajendra Kumar, Raj Kumar

Famous for: Being the highest-grossing Bollywood film of its time (taking $8.3 million worldwide) and for being the first Bollywood film to be nominated for an Academy Award (Oscar). It also has an amazing cult soundtrack.

2

Flames (Sholay)

Released: 1975

Starring: Amitabh Bachchan

Famous for: Being the only film in Bollywood history to be shown for 50 consecutive weeks across India. It is noted for its extraordinary mixture of comedy, action, music and dance – all the components of a classic Bollywood film.

The Big-hearted Will Take the Bride (Dilwale Dulhania Le Jayenge)

Released: 1995

Starring: Sharukh Khan, Kajol, Amrish Puri

Famous for: Setting a record of 750 weeks of continuous play in Mumbai, India, where it's still showing today!

Devdas

Released: 2002

Starring: Shahrukh Khan, Madhuri Dixit, Aishwarya Rai

Famous for: Being the most expensive Bollywood film ever made at the time of its release. It also earned ten Filmfare Awards, including individual awards for its stunning stars Shahrukh Khan and Aishwarya Rai.

5

Three Idiots

Released: 2009

Starring: Aamir Khan, R. Madhavan, Sharman Joshi

Famous for: Holding the record for the highest-grossing Bollywood film ever, taking just over $73.5 million! The film also showcases real inventions created by unknown people in their backyards!

HIGH DRAMA

The Bollywood look is glitzy, gorgeous and incredibly glam. Film stylists' must-haves include stunning clothes and dazzling jewellery. Glamorous hairstyles and head-turning make-up finish off the stunning 'film star' look.

Bollywood boys!

The hero of a Bollywood film is out to impress. High-action films may call for something modern but traditional clothes are still popular. If it's an all-out, spectacular Bollywood dance routine then expect to find the leading man in:

- kurta – a long shirt
- trousers – loose-fitting for extra kick
- sherwani – a long smart coat
- Nehru jacket – named after a former Indian prime minister, Nehru, the jacket has a rounded collar and was popular in the 1960s

The glitterati

Clothes are made from gorgeous fabrics including silk or taffeta. And no Bollywood outfit would be complete without glitter – lots of it! Beads, sequins and metallic, golden or silver threads are woven into the outfits for extra glamour.

Girls get glitzy!

Bollywood actresses wear beautiful costumes in an array of rich, vivid colours. Head to the wardrobe department on a Bollywood film set and you might find:

- saris – in hot, vibrant tones
- cholis – short tops, cropped above the waist
- trousers – loose-fitting so that dancers can move to the Bollywood beat
- chiffon tunics – with metallic threads woven into the fabric to add sparkle
- gold jewellery – plenty of bangles, earrings and ankle bracelets to shake and shimmer

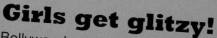

Finishing touches

Bollywood dancers have beautifully groomed hair. Women usually wear long, shiny hairpieces, which can be braided or woven with jewels. Most men go for neat, slicked back hair. Kohl eye make-up is a must and is sometimes worn by men, too. Women often wear a bindi, a dot or jewel on their forehead.

Colour codes

In India colours have different meanings, and Bollywood films sometimes use this symbolism. Red and gold are the colours for weddings. Yellow is usually for someone young and pure. Blue is popular for a beautiful woman and is often worn by the female lead in a Bollywood dance.

BEAT SPEAK

Spice up your Bollywood and bhangra speak with the Radar lingo guide!

bindi
a jewel or dot of make-up worn on the forehead

dhol
a traditional Indian drum used to play the main beat in bhangra music

Filmfare Awards
a ceremony held every year to award prizes to people who work in the Bollywood film industry

kurta
a loose-fitting, collarless shirt worn by many Indian men

Mumbai
the capital city of India

Nehru jacket
a man's Indian-style jacket with a short, high collar

sari
an Indian woman's dress-like garment made by wrapping fabric around the body

sherwani
a long coat worn by men. It was originally worn by kings or people of high rank in India in the eighteenth century

sitar
an Indian guitar used in bhangra and other traditional Indian music

sitar

GLOSSARY

breakdancing
a dance style normally performed to hip-hop music, with lots of acrobatic moves and ground work

component
a part of something

consecutive
following straight on from a previous event

cult
something that has achieved great recognition

epic
a particularly impressive or long story, usually featuring a hero or heroine

escapism
escaping reality through the imagination

exotic
different and unusual

extravaganza
an amazing show or display

folk dance
a traditional style of dancing which often originated in the rural areas of a country

fusion
a mixture of two or more influences

highest-grossing
taking the most money from the sale of tickets, DVDs and other merchandise

hip-hop
a style of music and dance that originated in the 1970s in the USA

independence
freedom from the rule of another person or another country

kohl
thick, black eye make-up

lavish
full and rich

mesmerising
something that is so interesting or exciting that the viewer cannot take their eyes off it

swinging 60s
a period of time in the 1960s when music, fashion and social attitudes went through exciting changes

symbolism
using an object, pattern or sign to represent an important or significant idea

troupe
a group of people who perform together

tunic
a shirt-like garment that is often worn with trousers

vibrant
exciting and rich

vivid
visually striking

BOP THIS WAY!

People to talk to

Exotic and exciting, Bollywood dance is also a great workout. If you want to add Bollywood and bhangra spice to your dance style here are a few organisations and dance schools to call:

Hina and Co Dance

Radar's very own Bollywood and bhangra expert dance teacher Hina Chavda runs fantastic dance courses and workshops. Find out more at:
www.hinaandcodance.com

Bollywood Vibes

Find out how to get a Bollywood dance workshop into your school at:
http://bollywoodvibes.co.uk

Simply Bhangra

If it's bhangra you're after, then the team at Simply Bhangra are on call:
www.simplybhangra.originationinsite.com

DVDs & Apps

Discover Bollywood through its movies, such as *Devdas* (2002) and *Singh is King* (2008).

If it's fun and fitness you fancy then why not give *Bollyrobics Dance Workout* (2009) a go. This DVD is guaranteed to raise a sweat and a smile.

Download the *Bollyrobics Dance Workouts* app and the *Top 100 Dance Hindi and Bollywood Songs* app from:
www.androidpit.com
www.itunes.com

INDEX